Waddie's Whole Load

WADDIE'S WHOLE LOAD
THE COWBOY POETRY OF WADDIE MITCHELL

Illustrated by the Author

GIBBS·SMITH
P
PUBLISHER

SALT LAKE CITY

First edition
97 96 95 94 7 6 5 4 3 2 1

Text and illustrations copyright © 1994 Waddie Mitchell

This is a Peregrine Smith Book, published by
Gibbs Smith, Publisher
P.O. Box 667
Layton, UT 84041

Design by J. Scott Knudsen / Waddie Mitchell
Cover photography by Steve Bunderson

Library of Congress Cataloging-in-Publication Data

Mitchell, Waddie, 1950–
    Waddie's whole load / Waddie Mitchell.
      p.   cm.
    ISBN 0-87905-608-8 (pbk)
    1. Cowboys—West (U.S.)—Poetry.   I. Title
PS3563.I825W3   1994
811'.54—dc20
                                    94–16502
                                        CIP

I dedicate this book to a great man
and a great friend, who will sure do to
ride the river with—Don Edwards.

Sometimes in one's life,
a person or a place
appeals so to one's inner self
that he makes himself
acquainted . . .

Honesty,
forthrightness,
steadfastness
are virtues each
worthy
of one's adoration—

I have found these in you
my friend,
and in so doing
have found them growing in me,
for I have now
an example.

Success is like a present
And can give your life a lift,
But if you get wrapped in yourself
It can be a sorry gift.

Contents

Life is like a singing river
That each one of us must ford,
And though our melodies may vary,
We often strike a common chord.
  —Waddie Mitchell

Whole Load

In a western town in the days of old,
'Fore the mine closed down for the lack of gold,
The folks there seized the oppertunity
An' built them a right smart community.

They built 'em a school where the "R"s were taught,
An' they built 'em a church on a corner lot,
An' they painted 'er white with a steeple high
To greet townsfolk as they's passin' by.

They had 'em a sheriff, a judge, an' a mayor,
But they needed a preacher to make things square.
So they sent back East, as was the general rule,
An' hired one fresh from divinity school.

When Sunday come, he was all decked out
To preach a sermon, whisper and shout;
But when he stepped out to the podium,
It was all too obvious that no one come

'Cept one old cowboy in a pew back there
In his Sunday shirt an' his greazed down hair.
He sat there quiet, just watched the floor,
With a 'ccasional glance toward the church's door.

Time stood still for the longest while
'Til the preacher coughed and faked a smile,
"Guess we could try it again next week."
But emotion reigned; he could hardly speak.

His demeanor was that of a scolded pup.
He turned to leave when old Jake spoke up:
"Now hold on there, Preacher, 'taint yer fault,
An' them there doors ain't like no vault,

"An' began to expound on the pearly gates . . ."

" 'Cuz thar ain't no locks for to keep folks out.
An' if you don't preach now, Satan's won the bout!
Now if I was to haul out a whole load a' hay
An' only one cow showed up, she'd git fed that day!"

Now this preachin' man, for the last few days
Had found it hard to cope with these western ways.
But he figured as how he'd found his call
From this profound man with this western drawl.

So he fixed his collar and stood up straight
An' began to expound on the pearly gates,
An' he amazed himself at his own recall
Of the book he waved—chapter, verse and all.

It was God Almighty's omnipotent power
That he lectured on for over an hour.
Then the wages of sin, and the hell's brim fire—
An' he didn't weaken an' he didn't tire.

He was jumpin' and screamin' and poundin' the floor
When he noticed ol' Jake weren't awake anymore.
Now, this made him mad an' he stomped to the pew,
He shook Jake's shoulder an' said, "I weren't through!
You're the one told me about that cow gettin' fed,
An' now here you're actin' like you're home in bed!"

"Yer right there, Preech, 'bout them things I told you.
An' if I'd that load of hay, it'd still hold true:
That cow would get fed, 'tis the cowman's code.
But I wouldn't feed her the whole dern load!"

Cat-astrophy

The other day in Santa Rosa
I had a chat with this ol' gent
And he shared with me a story.
This is somethin' how it went:

"This country here's where I was reared
Back in the early thirties.
I was just a teen and times were lean.
I was ridin' for McCurty's.
The spring was fun but the brandin' was done
And I reckons I'm back as a tramp,
But they offers me pay through the summer to stay
And ride at the Big Bottom Camp.
I thanks 'em kind, no never mind,
I'd be all by myself at the Bottom.
I figured, 'sides which, if I saved I'd be rich
When I finished up in the autumn.
What with fences to mend and cattle to tend
The work would keep me from getting too lazy,
But that cabin got tight in those hours at night
And began to drive me stir crazy.
Before long, I found I would talk just for sound;
Soon conversations would go on all night.
It weren't too bad, at first, but got increasingly worse—
I'd even argue with myself when I was right.
Then, one week I got a note, when my little sister wrote
That she was comin' out to see the camp and me.
She'd bring a pet to be my friend, and that would help to put an end
To my loneliness and lack of company.
When my sister arrived I was somewhat surprised.
To this day, I still think it's a pity:
Instead of bark and growl it was purrin' and meow—
It weren't no dog she brought; it was a kitty.
I was a little distraught at the present she brought,
But she argued the merits of a cat,

Said, "They don't whine or make a mess and they'll rid the house of pests."
So I figured that it might work out at that.
Well, I spent a lot of time kissin' up to that feline.
And I worked to build a bond with it each day.
But it didn't seem to care. It acted like I wasn't there,
Or like it'd rather have me go away.
I started thinkin' twice when it made friends with the mice,
When to me it'd never give a second look.
I was only there to tend its needs while it'd leave its dirty deeds
In my slippers or upon my favorite book.
Or, while asleep and in my bed, that cat would pounce upon my head.
And its food would have to be prepared just so.
But things had gone too far when I looked into my jar
And found hair and paw tracks in my sourdough.
So when I'd finally had enough, the decision wasn't tough:
I'd just divorce the pet my little sister brought.
So I threw the wench outside where I'd let that cat reside
With all my recent troubles—or so I thought.
But that scamp declared war every time I'd use the door,
And it would now and again win a bout.
It would fight its way inside, find a bran' new place to hide;
I'd spend hours to get that stupid cat back out.
Every day it got worse. I was startin' to curse
Just the thought of opening the door.
I was past gettin' mad. I'd dished out all I had,
But that cat would just come back for more.
It seemed to take pride in getting under my hide.
The work became my only buffer.
It would find some delight in keepin' me up all night,
Figurin' new ways in making me suffer.
So, with my esteem well abused and my patience all used
And my heart just about out of try,
I was left no recourse; I would use deadly force.
That kitty cat just had to die!
The problem was now in deciding just how.
I didn't want to just even the score,
So, I set out to devise that demon's demise.

It was revenge I was after—and more!
I was still in some doubt as to just how about
I was going to do ol' Pusser in.
I wanted it to be a cat atrocity,
Or, at the very least, a mortal sin.
So with murder on my mind, constantly I tried to find
The apparatus I would use to ring its knell.
Guns or knives just didn't seem harsh enough to fit the dream
Of the way I's gonna send it back to hell!
Then, on an open mountainside, one day I hapt to ride
Past the tunnel of a long-abandoned mine.
I stepped off to the ground and started rummaging around
To see what might be there that I could find.
I yelped like a fox when I looked in this box
And found some things that I knew I could use.
By a rusty ol' pick there lay a dry stick
Of powder and a coil of fuse.
You can imagine my delight! The puzzle fit together right.
It would be like I imagined the marines.
Stupid cats are quick to trust us. It would be poetic justice
When I'd blow it, in the morn, to smithereens.
So I let it in that night, as if I'd given up the fight,
And I chuckled to myself as vengeance loomed.
In a weird way it was fun. I'd let it gloat and think it'd won.
Little did it know that it was doomed!
I awoke as daylight broke. Despise and joy lumped in my throat
When I caught that cat and stuck it in a sack.
I left ajar the door, I needn't worry any more,
'Cuz I'd be the only one that's coming back.
I headed down the pasture, my ol' heart was beating faster.
You know, it's strange how crazed with hate a man can get.
My stride showed a persistence 'til I'd reached a good safe distance.
Now the time had come to blow this cat to bits!
So I tied the dynamite on the cat, secure and tight,
Then I struck a match and lit the fuse and run.
I hid behind a tree, got down upon one knee
And peeked around the trunk to watch the fun.

I was stunned and paralyzed when I saw and realized
That the cat weren't there where it had been before.
It was speeding up the trail like it was packin' precious mail
Straight for the house and towards that open door!
Before long I heard the blast. My world collapsed around me fast
As I realized I had just lost all I'd earned.
I just sat there on the ground analyzing what went down
And how cruel and fast the tables can be turned.
I finally trudged on up to see all the wreckage and debris.
There weren't much left that even could be saved.
But what made the whole thing worse—it was if I had been cursed—
That cat was fine and came through it unscathed.
The McCurtys promptly fired me as quick as they had hired me.
I'd lost my job and everything I owned.
I didn't draw a single cent for all those long, hard months I spent—
And all because I disliked being alone.

It's said dogs are more like men and that cats are feminine.
Remember that when you look for a lifelong friend.
Into marriage you're coerced, then it ends up in divorce,
And that cat will always get you in the end."

Well, that was the story he told me
About him and that summer's demise.
You know, age don't make men any smarter,
But an old man is generally wise.
I thanked him for the story he'd given
And I rose from my seat on the log,
And I'll always remember that cowpoke,
Old and alone—with his dog.

A braggart is much like a mutt dog,
'Cuz when all of his yelpin' is done,
If you'll watch him a little while,
He'll lick himself—with his tongue.

Puttin' Things Right

I am better having known her;
She helped shape who I am.
She welcomed me with open arms
Before I was a man.
She taught me how to just be me,
Be proud and stand up tall.
I can lose myself within her,
Or show her off to all.

And I miss her so this evening—
I'm obliged to be away.
We often don't know what we have
'Til once we start to stray.
Just the thought of her awaiting
Helps my heart to put things right,
And I've fallen in a state of Nevada tonight.

To spend a sunrise with her
Brings me joy untold;
Her independent nature
Lets me soar within her fold.
She's never tried to change me,
She's a pure and open mind.
The freedom that she offers
Secures the tie that binds.

And I miss her so this evening—
I'm obliged to be away.
We often don't know what we have
'Til once we start to stray.
Just the thought of her awaiting
Helps my heart to put things right,
And I've fallen in a state of Nevada tonight.

Her cow range beckons me to come
And ride it once again.
Her mountains lure my soul back
Where I communed with Him.
She's tempting me to go to town,
With glitz and neon lights,
And enticing me to sleep beneath
Her starlit desert nights.

And though I'm not there with her,
She's here within my heart;
Her influence is with me
Whenever we're apart.
But for now I'll just dream of her
And that helps to put things right
'Cause I've fallen in a state of Nevada tonight.

The Belle of the Ball

I drove her all right
To the shindig that night,
'Course I said it was just for the ride,
But it probably bought
Me some dances, I thought
As I walked with her proudly inside.

I paid our way in,
We got our hands stamped and then
I was ready to go shake a leg,
But we were met by some guys
With stars in their eyes
Before I'd hung my hat on a peg.

One asked, "May I Ma'am?"
And she offered her hand,
So I waved as they went off to dance,
And though she'd gone off with him,
I still thought with a grin,
Won't be long now 'til I get my chance.

By the wall were some chairs,
So I took a seat there,
And I marveled as she two-stepped around.
Her blonde hair would flow
As she danced to and fro,
Her feet barely touching the ground.

An hour slipped by;
There was no chance to try—
Seemed hopefuls were lined to the door.
But every once in a while
She would flash me a smile
As she waltzed past me out on the floor.

"Her feet barely touching the ground."

I was just going to go ask
When Miss Tucker come past—
All five foot and built somewhat round.
She insisted one whirl,
And I'll tell you, that girl
Purt near flung me plumb out of town!

I'd barely recouped
When Granny Coberri swooped
Me up for a varsouvienne.
Then a schottisch with Trish,
Who was once quite a dish—
But all things up . . . someday fall down.

It was becoming apparent,
With her full card I daren't
Even dream of a dance with her.
Besides, why would she
Want to waste time on me
When I was just one night's chauffeur?

So, except for one trip
To the truck for a nip,
I demoted myself to wallflower.
I watched two flasks abused,
And one fight defused,
And Miss Tucker make cowpunchers cower.

Seemed I sat there for days,
And tho' I'd try different ways,
I could not get close to her at all.
Don't know what I expect—
I guess that's what you get
When you come with the belle of the ball.

I wished I'd stayed at the ranch
As the band called "Last Dance!"
When I turned to see standing right there
By a whole herd of men
Doing their best to crowd in
Was that gal with the pretty blonde hair.

She winked me her charm,
Took 'holt of my arm.
All them fellers were sure looking sad
When she said through the noise,
"I'm real sorry, boys,
But the last dance I saved for my dad."

When someone is fishing for answers,
But for answering, you're not disposed,
Think of the fish that have never been caught
Because they just kept their mouths closed.

There's Nothin' Like Nothin'

'Twas their fourteenth Christmas together.
'Cept for the kids, he didn't have much to show
For the life he'd spent ridin' for cattle,
And he was feeling especially low.

For if ever a wife was obliging,
If ever a woman endured,
Then surely she was at the top of the list
And a gift from her man was deserved.

But he'd been kicked and was somewhat lame,
And a trip to the doc don't come free.
And extra money from startin' some colts
Don't get made with a busted-up knee.

Oh, the kids would get by with the trinkets they'd buy
From hair ropes he had traded in town,
And peanut brittle gold from Ma's recipe old
Would help weight little Christmas socks down.

But for her there was no silver package,
And that surely weighed heavy on he,
For this year, especially, he wanted
To have something for her 'neath the tree.

That night he said, "Dear, I've a question.
Would you come here by me and sit down?
Do you think I am wrong punchin' cattle,
And should I find me a good job in town?

"One that would make our life easier,
With good pay and benefits, too.
With two weeks vacation, a company car,
And a retirement plan when I'm through."

She smiled and put her arm 'round him,
Said, "You've worked yourself up in a stew.
There's nothin' like nothin' for Christmas,
When I get to share it with you.

"'Cuz you are the man that I wanted and chose
To live with 'til our days here are gone.
And one of the things that attracted me most
Was the lifestyle and ranches we'd live on.

"And that is as much a part of us now
As anything else is, for sure.
And to move us to town and lose what we have
Would be nothing but misery pure.

"So don't worry 'bout presents for Christmas,
And listen up, he-buckaroo,
There's nothin' like nothin' for Christmas,
When I know it's comin' from you."

Crownin' Glory

I'll touch upon a subject—
In case anybody cares—
That has to do, quite simply,
With the hat a cowboy wears.
It isn't called a "Cowboy Hat"—
That term is much confused.
But in designating origin,
It's "Western Hat" that's used.

Hat etiquette is simple,
As you might well suppose:
If you mess with someone's hat
Then you risk a broken nose.
It was once deemed improper
To wear it while you dine
Or while dancing with a lady—
But of late, I guess it's fine.

'Cuz no matter where you go,
There is the ever-present lack
Of a common apparatus
That is known as a hat rack!
It is not worn in the shower,
During anthems or to bed,
But for most things that you'll do,
It's fine to keep it on your head.

'Cuz there are sticky-fingered yahoos
Who would steal it from the spot
Where you left it in the corner
And then sell it, like as not.
Its style and its color,
Be it ten X or just four,
Is left to the discretion
Of the head it will adorn.

It finds its personality
With time and use and wear,
And it's worth the price you paid
To just not worry 'bout your hair!
But when you have that "crowning touch"
For all the world to see,
It tells them all that you relate
To our western history—
And that's big . . . and wild . . . and free!

Where To Go

A young cowboy went to his partner,
His mind was laid heavy with doubt.
He asked, "Could we visit a while, pard?
It's hard figurin' everything out.

"Some say my fire has too many irons,
There's not enough of me to go all around,
That I'm flyin' too high for my own good
And it's time I come back to the ground.

"Others say I need new direction,
That my pursuits have no real goal in mind,
There's other things I should be doing
That would be more deserving of time.

"But some think I've got something special,
And to go for it's all that's essential,
If I'd give it my time and my effort,
With hard work I might reach my potential."

His older friend squatted on haunches,
With a stick started scratching the earth,
Said, "Each man must make his own choices;
Free agency's given at birth.

"Your pendulum swings on inertia—
The proddin' and pullin's not needed.
You might lose your axis or even yourself,
If all advice given is heeded.

"You know, a dog in the woods, if he's healthy,
Is seldom hurt by one tick,
But if he's bit by too many or they hang on too long,
He'll soon find himself down and sick.

"Don't let threads be wound into cables;
Bust 'em now and set your mind free.
There's no one as able as you are
To pilot your own destiny.

"Now saddle up with the things that I've told you,
Leave man's little world far behind.
Find sanctuary out on the cow range.
Let the wind do its thing on your mind.

"Catch a good travelin' bronc, mustache his tail.
The time you spend out there won't scar.
Trot off 'cross the desert and search for that trail
That will help you find out who you are."

So he did, and while out where the cow roams,
He found most of the answers he sought,
And he came back contented—it all seemed so clear—
He would sow and reap his own lot.

See, the perspective he got 'gainst big country and skies
Made his problems seem really quite small
When he compared 'em to the size of this world
And the intricate scheme of it all.

So the moral to this little story
Is when your mind is all clouded with doubt,
Go out on the mountain to ponder—
It's there that you'll figure things out.

Peg-Leg Pig

It'd been a while since I'd seen him
   So I stopped at his abode.
      I was plenty hot and thirsty
         From the desert miles I'd rode.

He poured our cups full to the brim.
   We sat there in the shade
      Upon a wobbly old parson's bench
         And sipped our lemonade.

We visited a while about neighbors
   And the poor price cattle were bringing,
      About the war and the friends we'd lost,
         And the dung the politicians were slinging.

I finished my cup; he again poured it full,
   When this pig, minus one hind leg,
      Hobbled on by, just as nice as you please
         With the use of a tailor-made peg.

"Well, I declare, I never knew
   You had a heart so big
      To take the time to whittle out
         A stump for a legless pig."

"That's no common critter, pard,
   And I am here to say,
      If it woren't for that there lagless pig,
         I wouldn't be here today."

That draws my interest, and he goes on to say
   How he was sleepin' real good one night
      When he's awoke from his slumbers by some hideous squeals—
         That pig's causin' a terrible fright.

"Well, I declare . . ."

"Well, I grabs for my gun to silence his noise
  When I realize I'm just about fumed;
    The house is afire! I dives through the door,
      Moments later, the whole place is consumed.

"Twas that pig's oinkin' and squealin's
  What got me out of my bed,
    And if it wasn't for him,
      I'd be standin' here dead!"

"Well, I see how your life
  Might have been shorter
    If it weren't for that there pig.
      How'd he lose that hind quarter?"

"Hold on there, pard,
  You ain't heard the whole story.
    Why, he saved me again
      On my own lower forty.

"See, I was draggin' the meadow
  With my ol' Poppin' John;
    I's gonna cross this here ditch,
      But my angle was wrong.

"The tractor tipped over,
    Pinned me to the ground
        Right there in the ditch.
            I thought I was drowned!

"But that pig started rootin'
    The ground beneath me
        Till he loosened my leg—
            And that set me free."

Well, after listenin'
    To my friend's testimony,
        I reckoned this pig's smarter
            Than the Lone Ranger's pony.

"Is that how he lost
    His hind leg?" I inquired.
        "Or was it when he saved you
            From that terrible fire?"

He looked at me then
    Like I was some sort of dunce,
        Said, "Man, you don't eat a good pig like that—
            All at once!"

So Darn Hard

It happens all too often in this current day and age,
Through mistakes and poor decisions that are made along the way,
From a small misunderstanding, soon a full-scale war's engaged,
And we find one day that . . . we're alone.

So we put on a good front and we divvy up the blame,
And we dig ourselves a pit so we can wallow in our pain.
And we doubt if we will ever find the nerve to try again,
Because it didn't work at all . . . together.

But it's so darn hard to be alone,
To be out there in this cold world on your own,
To be apart from everything that is comf'terble and known.
Oh, it's so darn hard to be alone.

But somehow we carry on and we keep the tears at bay,
And we hold tight to our sanity and live life day to day.
And we don't go off the deep end though our life's in disarray.
But it's so darn hard . . . to be alone.

Then we bottle up our fear and we grab another gear,
And we give it one more try although the future's left unclear.
But it's said that all good things will come to those who persevere—
And we try it once more . . . with another.

'Cuz it's so darn hard to be alone,
To be out there in this cold on your own,
To be apart from everything that is comf'terble and known.
Oh, it's so darn hard to be alone.

How come a man with no knowledge wants to share it,
And it's those standing near who have to bear it?

A Ray of Hope

I'd been ridin' for a living since I started drawin' wages,
Workin' outfit after outfit, crossin' bridges, turnin' pages,
Been on crews where just to make it back to camp with most my hide
After workin' cows or horses reaped a misled source of pride.

Was of the mind that 'less I fought 'em and the bronc and I was wrung
That I hadn't conquered nothin' 'cuz no battles had been won.
Used to roll 'em in the saddle, quirt and spur 'em on the rise,
And I'd really earned my wages when defeat showed in their eyes.

I came to hide my fears behind the mask of fakin' I was tough,
An' makin' up for lack of knowledge with a superficial bluff.
Then into my world a man rode with a new philosophy,
Said if my horse was havin' troubles, they most likely start with me.

Well, at first my neck hairs bristled at the bluntness of the thought
And I steamed around there thinkin', gosh, the nerve that feller's got!
But that night my heart recounted all the many things he told—
I guess ideas pass from head to head but truth enters the soul.

And the next thing that he said made more than just a little sense,
"Remember, every kind of animal has some intelligence,
And it's up to us to figure how to tap into that vein:
Some of us will use suggestion, while there are others who'll use pain.

"Let's say if every time I wanted your attention, there's no doubt
I could get it if I took a quirt and smacked you on the snout.
And before too long, I'm guessin', just the threat of that there quirt
Would have you jumpin' sideways just to keep from gettin' hurt.

"Then I could say that I accomplished all that I set out to do,
Because I'm sure I'd get response to anything I asked of you.
But if your opinion then was asked, I doubt it'd take you very long
To spell out with much conviction everything I's doin' wrong.

"But on the other hand, if I was to approach you as a friend,
And then explain what I was tryin' to accomplish in the end
And give you a chance to understand each thing I asked of you—
We'd be pardners in the venture and content when we were through.

"It's worth much more than we invest to gain that kind of friendship,
Should we ever strike that harmony that builds a lasting kinship.
But if you feel it's just not worth the time you'd have to spend,
Then you should find a different job that'd make you happy in the end."

Well, I agreed with what he said, so I asked him to tell me more,
And he said, "Horses are like people and require a rapport.
Every one is individual; we can't treat them all the same.
We must recognize their differences to find that common plane.

"But when we accept the challenge of tryin' to educate,
We can't assume every student's going to learn at the same rate
Or to receive from them respect, for that's something that we must earn—
Keep a pupil's interest high and the more readily they'll learn.

"They'll ingest things even faster if we keep their minds at ease,
For the more they like their schoolin', all the more they'll want to please.
So our goal should be to try to keep the horse from feelin' stressed,
For we want them working naturally and under no duress.

"While some respond quite easily to a certain thing we ask,
To another, it's a 'booger' and he'll take us quick to task
To alleviate the 'getcha' that he's found there in his way.
If we don't, it holds up progress down the road another day.

"Let's say my pony throws his head and bonks me on the crown—
Do you think I'd cure the problem if I simply tied it down?
It would keep his head from tossin'—which would help me feel secure—
But I'd be bandaging a symptom with a temporary cure.

"I could save a wreck on down the line for me and for the horse
If I'd take the time to pinpoint the real trouble at its source,
Because the best approach I've found is to attack the problem's core.
It takes much time to heal a wound if we don't medicate the sore."

And he talked about the other sense that's still within our reach
That very few develop 'cuz we rely so much on speech:
"If we're alert to body language and the aura they convey
We can know the horse's feelin's through the 'silent other way.'

"We must reward an honest effort, recognize the smallest tries
Trust our feel, forget the gimmicks, open up our mind and eyes.
Never set a limit on a horse—we don't know where he'll crest.
Think ahead, set situations, stretch to draw the pony's best.

"But never ask for more than they have the ability to give
Or their willingness to try will drain like water from a sieve.
It's a fine line that we're walkin', but a noble one, for sure.
If we put ourselves into the horse's place, how much could we endure?

"The game of discipline we're playin' must be dealt the same each round.
If we change the rules in midstream, what we're strivin' for might drown.
They will want to play the simple way; bad habits they'll discard
If we make the right things easy, what we don't want done seem hard.

"When we're sittin' in the saddle, it's up to us to stay aware
Of what's goin' on beneath us, show them that we really care,
Learn to feel where every foot is placed and to cue accordingly.
We can't expect to have it done right 'less we know how it should be."

Then he spoke of phantom barricades that I'd bump up against
When a problem comes along that I'd not yet experienced.
He assured me they'd be nothing more than walls my mind construed,
And the best way to get past them is to sit and think them through.

I once asked where he acquired all the know-how that he's got.
He paid homage to his mentor who had shared this train of thought.
He said, "Man has pooled his knowledge; from that well it's easily drawn.
And one of mankind's duties is to try to pass it on."

There were times that I misunderstood something that he had said,
And I'd set my jaw and argue 'til my face and neck were red.
But when I'd finally get a grasp, he'd assure me with a wink.
Guess in essence what he taught me was to practice how to think.

End results would prove his teaching are of solid base and sound,
Not just idealistic notions that could not get off the ground.
And they expand way past the confines of the "bronco bustin' pen"
To other facets of one's life and the relationships therein.

His motives seek no credit, notoriety or fame.
But for us, who's out there playin', he's the leader of the game.
His time with me was too short, but I am thankful to this day
That there's men like him in this world—and he happened by my way.

You've got to be so careful
'Cause one never really knows,
When an injury's inflicted,
Where eventually it shows.
My words were meant to bring good cheer,
But how was I to tell
That praise I'd utter in his ear
Would cause his head to swell?

One Christmas in West Texas

'Twas the night before Christmas on the West Texas plain,
The ranch had been suffering for a much-needed rain.
Still, spirits were high when kids bedded that night,
While their mother and I were assessing our plight.
We'd figured for hours the money we'd need
To sustain the cattle with supplement feed;
Our figures confirmed we would have to sell out
If there soon wouldn't come an end to the drought.
Resigned to these facts, we arose from the table
To put out the few gifts our small budget made able—
The bounty this year would be pitif'ly small—
When we noticed a note that'd been tacked on the wall.
It read, "Please, dear Santa, we'd rather you'd bring,
Instead of some toys, just one special thing:
Some rain for the country so the grass can grow tall.
We think that would be the best present of all—
Might keep us from havin' to move from this place."
Then I noticed their mom wipe a tear from her face.
"We're blessed in spite of our troubles," she said.
We hugged and held hands as we went off to bed.
We were wakened at dawn by some young shouts of glee:
"Mommy! Daddy! Please hurry, come see!
We knew he was real and would hear our request,"
As they pointed to heavy black clouds to the west.
We were yelling and laughing and dancing around
When the first precious drops started hittin' the ground.
Then all of a sudden, the clouds seemed to burst,
While the soil was quenchin' its powerful thirst.
From that Christmas on our whole family will claim
That the best present ever was a West Texas rain.

Story With a Moral

I know there's things worse
      that make cowpunchers curse,
And I reckon it's happened to us all.
Though it's been years, since, you can bet,
      when I think of it yet,
It still makes my old innards crawl.

I was making a ride
      to bring in one hide
That hadn't showed up in the gather;
I was riding upstream,
      daydreaming a dream,
When I caught there was something the matter.

Near some quaking asp trees,
      I had caught in the breeze
A stench that was raunchy and mean,
And I reckoned as how
      it might be that old cow,
So I rode to a bend in the stream.

Sure enough, that cow lied
      in the creek there and died.
Hard telling how long she'd been there.
She was bloated and tight—
      was a horrible sight!
She was oozing and slipping her hair.

Her eye sockets were alive
      with maggots that thrive
On dead flesh, putrid yellow and green,
An' the hot sun burning down,
      turnin' pink things to brown,
Spewing oily gunk in the stream.

I spurred upwind fast
      to get away from the blast
Of the heavy stink that cow made.
And I felt bad seein's how
      I had lost the old cow,
So I pulled up near a tree in the shade—

Then, I got sick to the core,
      rememberin' just moments before
I'd done something that made me feel worse:
Not thirty yards down,
      I'd stepped off to the ground
And drank till my belly near burst!

For months after it,
      just the thought made me spit,
And I'd live it over like a bad dream.
And the moral, I think,
      is if you must take a drink,
Never, ever remount and ride upstream.

Typical

Out on the cliff's edge further than he'd ever been before
He sat with legs a danglin' high above the valley's floor.
He was lost in thought while drinking in the grandeur of it all,
When a gust of wind unseated him and he began to fall.
'Twas a drastic situation and he didn't dare think slow,
For certain death awaited in the rocky crags below.
So he called upon a friend (I guess the only one he could)—
The one we all forget about when things are going good.
He said, "God, if you will help me now, I'll quit my sinful ways;
I will do those things you'd have me do and work hard all my days;
I will quit the booze and cigarettes and help my loving wife;
I will spend time with my children and I'll turn around my life;
I will work to help the needy and I promise to repent."
Just then, a tree limb caught his coat and stopped his fast descent.
And while hanging from the tree that grew upon that rocky shelf
He looked skyward saying, "Never mind, I handled it myself!"

"Just then, a tree limb
caught his coat and
stopped his fast descent."

Vows

written for a friend's wedding

HIM
I stand and look you in the eye
And make some vows that I'll live by.
They're not some laws that's been decreed,
But things I think we both will need
To help this union stand the test—
A code, like we live by out West.

First, respect I'll freely share,
Like man with bronc, it must be there.
Next, the precious gift of time
Will now be ours, and not just mine,
To spend together, which is only right,
Like a cowboy's wages on a Saturday night.

And I swear today on this wedding ring,
That I'll see to your needs as I would my string.
Keep you shod and groomed, and amply fed,
Tend to your needs 'fore I hit the bed.
So as we travel this trail of life,
You'll have cause to be happy in being my wife.

HER

I, too, today some vows will make,
Realizing marriage is give and take.
I'll trade my inner thoughts with you
And share the dreams you'd want me to.
We'll stay together through thick and thin;
I'll be your partner, mate, and friend.

Like the camptenders I've grown to admire,
I'll tend to our love like they do the fire.
I'll add fuel and stoke it and watch over it right,
So it will burn hot through the longest of nights.
It will never go out for my lack of care.
It's my number one job, and I'll always be there.

They'll hitch us today together as one,
To pull the same burden, to share the same fun.
So if they pull a wet collar pad off of you,
They'll pull a wet collar pad off me, too.
Whether travelin' a level, or a steep rocky road,
I'll not have you pullin' the heavier load.

Cynical

I was young and new at life's game,
I'd been sheltered from the world.
He was fifteen years my senior,
And I'd found myself the girl
That I hoped to live my life with,
But unsure of what to do.
I asked for his advice.
And he said, "Son, let me tell you—

"First, get some education,
Then establish a career;
Save all your hard-earned money;
Never shift out of high gear.
Go buy a house and car,
Some stocks and lots of property,
Then give it to a gal you hate
And skip the misery."

His cynicism shocked me,
And I thought it rather sad
That a man could be so jaded
With a heart so very mad.
So my convictions just got stronger:
I could prove his outlook wrong,
And with the right girl as my mate,
I'd never sing his woeful song.

"First, get some education,
Then establish a career;
Save all your hard-earned money;
Never shift out of high gear.
Go buy a house and car,
Some stocks and lots of property,
Then give it to a gal you hate
And skip the misery."

So I cleared my mind of bad thoughts,
And I planned a blissful life.
Then I got down on my knee
And asked that girl to be my wife.
Now it's been twelve years come next month
Since we had our wedding day,
And if a young man comes to me
For some advice, here's what I'll say:

"First, get some education,
Then establish a career;
Save all your hard-earned money;
Never shift out of high gear.
Go buy a house and car,
Some stocks and lots of property,
Then give it to a gal you hate
And skip the misery."

Harsh Words

If you face an altercation
With your family, spouse or friend—
And what you say just might determine
How things turn out in the end—
Hold a tight rein on emotions;
Keep them checked at any cost,
For they can stampede all your senses
And a temper's easily lost.

Weigh the words that you'll use carefully;
Think of how they'll be perceived.
For once they're said, your grip's released,
And they can never be retrieved.
For there is no spell or recipe
To conjure cruel words back.
And of burdens we must carry,
Regrets are heaviest to pack.

But harsh words never spoken
Can't show up to haunt one day.
You determine what you'll harvest
From seeds you sow along your way.
Friendship is too important,
And good ones too far between.
Bonds won't be torn by difference,
But sharp tongues will cut them clean.

When you claim you're tired of livin' alone
But to find a good woman's too tuff,
Remember,
Even a blind dog sometimes finds a bone
If he just sniffs around long enough.

Commutin'

There ain't nothin' like the feelin'
Thet ya git down deep inside
As ya trot out in the mornin'
When you've hired on to ride

And your mount's enthusiastic
And the air is crisp and new
And there's lively conversation
Goin' on amongst the crew.

There's some bridle crickets chirpin',
Jingle bobs tap out a tune;
On one side the sun is risin',
Just ahead there sets the moon.

Shadows high trot there beside ya,
Elongated, keepin' pace,
Reassurin' you ain't hobbled
By restrictive time or space.

Out in front the boss is postin'
To the same beat as his song,
And the realization hits ya
That you're right where you belong.

It's then you start appreciatin'
You're on trails where few have trod.
Wonder how you ever doubted
If there really is a God.

Atop a ridge the boss reins in,
So we gather up around;
It's from here he'll call the circle,
So you step off to the ground.

Ya loosen up the latigo
An' air your pony's back;
You arrange again the blankets
And ya realign your kack;

You mount back up then get dropped off,
Check to see who's on each side.
You're glad that you're a cowboy
And you feel a twinge of pride.

Ya ate breakfast by the Coleman,
Hurried 'round to beat the sun,
Have eleven miles behind ya,
But it's here the work's begun.

Now, in town when folks must travel
To their workplace every day,
It's said that they're commuting
To their job to earn their pay.

They choke in crazy traffic jams,
Fight for seats on bus or train.
It's a wonder that this ritual
Doesn't drive them all insane.

We, too, I guess, commute to work
As the job at hand dictates,
But we commune while we're commutin'—
And what a difference that makes.

"Shadows high-trot there beside ya . . . "

No Second Chance

Did you ever wish you could turn time back
      and live things over again
To abort regrets or bite a lip
      so as not to hurt a friend?
You could pull up your horse before he fell
      (that steer still got away);
Or push a little harder when the works went bad
      so the job'd get done that day?

You could back up and listen to your granddad's tales;
      they're buried with him now.
You could even say "No" when your pa asked, "Son,
      wanna learn to milk a cow?"
You could take the time to help your son,
      maybe train his pup,
Or teach him that no good will
      come from ever givin' up.

And the colt that bucked in the rocks that day
      mightn't if your temper hadn't flared;
If you'd have figured out where his mind was at,
      you'd a known that the bronc was scared.
If we could just but relive time,
      our lives would be enhanced.
But best try to do it the first time 'round,
      'cuz there ain't no second chance.

When a politician's spewing forth
Excuses to a crowd,
Remember,
When shaken, full barrels are silent,
But near-empties rattle loud.

Don

I saw emotions well up in him
As she pointed with a grin,
Saying, "Sign there at the bottom, please,"
While handing him a pen.

I could tell he needed venting
Or I feared he would explode;
So, I dug in for the onslaught
While he proceeded to unload
His opinions on that young gal;
How this country should be run;
How lawyers should be something scarce;
And how business should be done.

How you didn't need no contracts
When a man's word was an oath,
And it was worth a lot more
Than a paper signed by both.

How at one time giant deals were made
With the shaking of a hand,
And you could bet your life and livelihood
On the promise of a man.

How neighbor meant a whole lot more
Than simply living near;
And all could walk the streets at night
Without a nagging fear.

How citizens could arm themselves
And crimes weren't blamed on guns
But on crimesters that committed them,
And bad ones still got hung.

How a shyster's reign was short-lived
'Cause good folks would run them off,
And thugs and thieves would land in jail
'Cause judges weren't so soft.

How divorce was near unheard of,
And kids were raised at home;
How there weren't no old-folks' centers
'Cause we took care of our own.

How cars and tools weren't throw-away
'Cause things were built to last.
How a man would tip his hat out
On the street when ladies passed.

The young gal's eyes were glazin'
As she stood there in a stare.
I was gettin' kind of antsy
And was wantin' out of there—

But he went on about . . . fat cowboys—
How they once were hard and lean
Before they all used trucks and goosenecks—
And how strikes were seldom seen.

How you didn't need no resumé
To land yourself a job;
How public office wasn't just
A legal way to rob;

How if you were able-bodied
Then you found yourself some work,
And welfare wasn't handed out
To lazy bums that shirk.

How doctors still made house calls
That didn't cost an arm and leg;
How an appointment with your banker
Wouldn't dictate that you beg.

How insurance was affordable
'Cause people weren't so apt to sue;
How you didn't expect ten times more
Than you were rightf'ly due.

How taxes didn't break ya
'Cause we all paid our fair share,
And there weren't folks spendin' full time
Finding all the loopholes there.

How the public trough weren't feedin'
Near as many bureaucrats;
And when the BLM was small—
But now they're like a swarm of gnats.

How credit cards are rip-offs;
How voters have got to learn
That you can't pay off a deficit
If you spend more than you earn.

How if somebody is strugglin'
We should lend a helping hand.
How it ain't right that some foreigners
Are buying up this land.

He'd gone on for twenty minutes
Before he took hisself a breath.
I thought I'd better jump in now
'Fore he talks that gal to death.

So, I said, "Don, you're right on all counts,
But we've really got to go—
And if you don't sign that there contract,
We can't rent the video!"

Rodeo

We're all here to see a rodeo—
A tradition of the West.
It's the purest kind of drama,
Competition at its best,
Pitting cowboys, stock and stopwatch
In the arena here today
To a grueling exhibition
And a fabulous display
Of wrecks and rides and fortitude—
Excitement from the start—
Of emotions, luck and attitude,
Of passion, skill and heart.

It's unique in every aspect—
An American prodigy,
Having roots so firmly planted
In our country's history.
It is family entertainment;
It has danger lurking near.
You'll see results of endless practice;
You'll see triumph over fear;
You'll see horses and their riders
Work together as if one;
You'll see the agile contradictions
Of bucking bulls that weigh a ton.

The athletes competing
Are the heroes here today.
Some had eggs for breakfast,
And some a flake of hay.
And the cowboys and the cowgirls
And the stock will all agree
That if asked about their druthers
There's no place they'd rather be.
And they're here to do their level best
To give you folks a show,
So hold onto your hats
Because it's time to rodeo!

Difference

For years I heard, while growin' up,
'Bout the difference in cowboy styles
An' figured the difference 'tween strict wrong or right
Was a region, or in some cases, just miles.

How one group of fellers were all off their track
An' were doomed to suck a hind tit,
'Cuz they used double rigs and their ropes were too short
And they used a grazer-type bit.

Or if, Lord forbid, they'd use split leather reins
Or a breast collar hung on their kack
You could be sure all their mounts would be hard in the mouth,
And galled on their withers or back.

And stories were told how the fellers down south
Would tie off their ropes to the horn.
To the dallie tradition I'd growed up with
Those stories brought nothing but scorn.

An' when I was sure I'd grown up in the place
That done most everything best,
Fate dealt me a hand to start travelin' some,
So I left "perfect" to work with the "rest."

When I hit Arizona, the brush poppers there
Just laughed at my long tapaderos,
The sixty-foot "gut" I had braided myself
And my respect for the old-time vaqueros.

They were gatherin' remnants an' were tied hard and fast,
And they worked clean and slick for their pay,
And though I got along, if I'd stayed for a year,
I'm sure I'd have been doing it their way.

On her prairie and in her mountains,
I rode Colorado's range,
And with her scrub oak and pine trees and toolies
Some of my ways had to change.

From Wyoming to Montana to Texas,
I learned something each place that I went;
And though I found my way back to Nevada,
I think my time gone was well spent.

'Cause I learned that there's plenty good cowboys
Scattered throughout the great West,
And the way that they work and the gear they use
For their circumstances seems to be best.

And I've noticed that most all good cowboys
Take pride in their saddle and tack,
An' though they vary in how fancy they're built,
It's a must that they don't hurt a back.

An' as for the head gear their horses will wear—
Though I like mine silver inlaid—
You can bet it's high quality and won't hurt a horse
Be it grazer bit, snaffle, or spade.

Now I'm not sayin' they were all good cowboys,
And there's gunsils where I come from, too,
Seems their rule for the tack that they'll use
Is: "As long as it's cheap, it'll do."

But the cow range ain't lacking good cowboys
And their problem's the same as we have here:
It's an ever-increasing difficult time
In finding high-quality gear.

So here's to the cowboy craftsmen—
Those few who keep standards up high,
Who'll take the time and the effort
To make the best gear that money can buy.

Be it silver, metal, saddles, or boots,
Canvas, or felt, or rawhide—
These are the folks who make all the stuff
That is feed for a cowpuncher's pride.

Shorty

When I first met up with Shorty
I was sixteen and abrupt,
I'd been raised 'round cows and horses,
Thought I knew which way was up.

I'd landed a job at the Seven S,
Hired out to buckaroo,
Was to pull out with the wagon,
And this Shorty was on the crew.

He was old already,
Little, thin, and unassuming,
And the flame that burned his passion
For this cowboy life was all-consuming.

And I can't help but remember,
As I sit here and reflect,
How this man who wore the Blanchard spurs
Had gained the crew's respect.

At night sometimes he'd talk about
His mother, school, and home,
And how at fourteen years of age
He'd set out on his own.

How he'd aimed to be a cowboy
And had worked free for a ranch
Mucking stalls and digging postholes
'Til he'd earned himself a chance.

How he'd worked in Arizona
Popping brush and tyin' off,
Spending winters on a camp job
Where the trails were awful rough.

How he'd come out to Nevada
Where he'd spent these many years,
But when he'd think again of Mother
His eyes would fill with tears.

For he'd say, "I never made it back
To see her 'fore she died,"
And regrets he had about that
Were impossible to hide.

I just thought him sentimental,
Old and foolish in his ways.
See, being young, I thought life was
An endless wealth of days.

He'd talk of wagons and cowboys
And different ranches he'd rode on,
But his stories seemed prehistoric
'Cause now most of them were gone.

He'd talk of friends he'd like to see
And places that he'd been,
And how, come fall, he'd take some time
And visit them again.

But something always happened
And he'd never really go,
Except his yearly junket
To the Denver Livestock Show.

'Cause work and life tied Shorty down
Doing things he thought he should.
There just weren't time to get around
Like he'd always wished he could.

And on occasion he'd get word
That some ol' pal had died.
He'd say "Damn, I could have seen him,
But I didn't really try."

And if that feller's name come up
In a story later on,
Shorty'd pause and blink a tear
And say, "I really should have gone."

In the paper yesterday
It hurt me when I read
That Shorty Daniels passed away
While sleeping in his bed.

I got those feelin's that ya get
When a pardner's soul's been freed
And I knew we'd lost another
Of the last few of a breed.

I'd heard how Shorty had been sick
And wasn't doing well,
And figured I would take some time
And visit him a spell.

But, well, I never made it
Before ol' Shorty died.
Damn, I could have seen him,
But I didn't really try.

Then my memories started wanderin'
Back to other pals I've missed,
And it got a little scary
As I made a mental list.

And it made me start to think about
Some things on my back shelf—
Like friends I haven't seen for years;
How history repeats itself.

How outfits that I've worked on
Have sold out and are no more.
And I'm startin' now to understand
What Shorty choked up for.

I suppose it's in the scheme of things,
And we all have our regrets,
And I reckon it's just one more thing
That living life begets,

But I bet when Shorty's name comes up
In a story later on,
I'll likely pause and blink a tear
And say, "I really should have gone."

There's so many sons'a-bitches
That spew environmental wrath,
That ranchers feel like they're a hydrant
Placed beside a "doggie" path.

Christmas at the Cross

We were camped at the Cross
Where the buckaroos stayed
In the winter, kind of out of the way
Of the rosin-jaws' sight
With their wagons and teams
In the days when men forked all the hay.

We were ridin' the feed grounds
And doctor'n a few
But shackin' up when the weather got strong.
There were six of us there,
Varying greatly in age,
But by an' large all the crew got along.

The holiday season
Was on us again,
With festivities startin' around,
And the bunkhouse was busy
With five buckaroos
Sprucin' up for the big dance in town.

All but Charley was goin',
An' I didn't understand,
So I look over at Jim and I say,
"What's wrong with Ol' Charley?
He ain't comin' again.
Is he scroogin' this great holiday?"

"I've noticed that, too,"
Was Jim's quick reply.
"He's been about as much fun as a bone.
And lately, durin' our
Bull sessions at night,
He's been locked in his room all alone."

"I've seen it, too.
He's been actin' some strange,"
We were both interrupted by Ron.
"I got up in the night
Sometime last week
And the light in his room was still on."

"Let him brew in himself
An' just leave him be,"
Harold said with a jig in his gait.
"It's time we was headin'
In town to the dance
To show the girls how we all celebrate!"

"These guys are all calling you
Scrooge, Charley boy.
Better come dance'n and prove 'em all wrong."
"Thanks, Gary, but no,"
Was Charley's reply.
"You boys best be gettin' along."

It was 'long in the mornin'
'Fore we made it back home
On that Christmas day long ago,
With our blistered feet
An' our heads in a fog
An' a new six inches of snow.

Charley met us with a smile
An' a spring in his step
That he made sure none of us missed.
"Good mornin', fellas
I'll tend to the chores.
Oh, by the way, Merry Christmas."

"He's rubbin' it in,"
I thought to myself
As I went down the hall to my room.
All I could think of
Was the day off in bed
To help me get over this gloom.

I flopped on my tarp,
Not bother'n to
Even rid myself of my coat.
My stomach's a mess
And my head's throbbin' now,
An there's a blow torch lit up in my throat!

In addition to the discomfort
I already felt,
I laid on something that made my face hurt,
So I push myself up,
Try to focus my eyes
To see a bran' new rawhide quirt.

It was of curious workmanship,
Shot loaded to boot,
An' balanced just right for my hand.
My name was on a tag
That was tied to the lash
Signed by "Santa, the jolly ol' man."

In a dumbfounded stupor
I go to the hall
To see Jim look'n dumb as a bell.
He was holdin' a real nice
Mane-hair mecate
With slobber straps tooled up real well.

Then out came Harold,
Then Gary, then Ron—
All holdin' gifts from Ol' St. Nick.
Each piece was handcrafted
Especially for him,
And each man thought that his was the pick.

"So this is what he's
Been doin' of late,"
Harold said. "We should all be ashamed.
Why, he's give of his talents,
Effort and time,
And didn't even sign his own name."

"Here we all thought
He's been actin' like Scrooge
'Cuz some dancin' and parties he's missed.
While all of the goodwill
We've all shown combined,"
Gary moaned, "wouldn't start a small list."

Well, about that time
Charley comes through the door,
Havin' done all the chores for the day.
And there in the hall
Stood five hung-over punchers
Gulpin' hard to find something to say.

"I'll shoe your string for you."
"I'll oil your rig."
"I'll wrangle your turn for six weeks."
"Now hold on there, boys,
I didn't do this for that.
You've just all got a case of the meeks.

"If you'll give me a minute
And open your ears,
Stop feelin' you should do somethin' for me,
I'll tell you my motives—
They're selfish as hell—
If you try it someday you might see.

"As you know, I never married
Nor had me no kids;
'Twas a saddle I chose for my life.
But I'm older now,
And my ideas have changed,
And I regret never takin' a wife.

"But be as that may,
I've learned to live
With the situation I've bought,
And in the last few years
I've come to realize
That you're the only family I've got.

"So a few years ago,
For the first time in my life,
I give of myself—just a bit.
An' the rewards that I got
From them good feelin's inside
Was more than I dreamed I would get.

"So now I look forward
Each year to the time
When I get to play Santa's elf,
An' do a little somethin'
For the folks I hold dear,
Thus assurin' rewards for myself."

Well, that was the last Christmas
I ever spent around Charley,
But I'm sure I will never forget it,
For that was the year
Five of us buckaroos
Learned a little about true Christmas spirit.

Except maybe for Alaska,
This new tax reform we've got
Is perhaps the biggest snow job
That our country's ever bought.

Bet at the Bar

It's said every story has a hero,
Or at least one character that's main,
But to call Larry anything less than grotesque
Is borderin' on the insane.

In a tavern booth in the days of my youth,
We sat wastin' away precious time;
And one day what ensued—though you may think it crude—
Is the plot for this story in rhyme.

See, Larry liked to bet, an' he yelled where he set
In a voice that was screechy and high,
**"Hey, Barkeep, I will bet a ten-dollar bill
I can bite my own right eye."**

Now this 'Keep, overgrown, for bein' congenial weren't known,
And his conversation often lacked grace.
And all the hours therein that we'd spent in that den
We never once saw a smile on his face.

He glared at our friend with an evil-like grin.
I sure didn't think he would buy it,
But he reached in the till and pulled out a bill,
Said, *"I'd like to see you try it!"*

Well, Larry popped out his glass eye and bit it, not hard,
Then returned the thing to its socket.
Then he picked up his winnin', all the time widely grinnin',
An' stuck it neat in his pocket.

Some cuss words were said, the 'Tender's face it turned red,
'Tweren't hard seein' he wasn't too tickled.
Larry saw the despise in his bloodshot eyes,
An' grinned that grin he grins when he's pickled.

"You best leave while you've still got a face."

"You're a strange sort of bloke, most folks laugh at that joke,
But you didn't," Larry says with a sigh.
"But, I'm of sportin' men, so I'll bet one more ten
I can bite my own left eye."

"You couldn't be blind, I myself seen you find
Your way through tables enroute to the john.
You're trying a bluff; think I've not guts enough—
Well, I'm callin' your hand, Kid, you're on!"

Now Larry weren't blind, that was easy to see,
And that 'Keep thought he'd found his reprieve,
So he flopped down a ten spot and folded his arms,
But Larry had a trick up his sleeve.

See, Larry'd been kicked in the mouth as a kid
By a horse he was tryin' to bite,
And what few teeth were left after that episode
Some years later were lost in a fight.

This time he didn't pop out any glass peeper—
Though he acted like he give it a try—
But with a toothless grin of a man richer by ten,
He used his false teeth to bite his left eye.

The Bartender blew, cussed Larry clean through,
Said, *"Take the money and git out of this place.*
I've been swindled today and you've got most my pay,
You best leave while you've still got a face."

"I assure you, Sir, 'twas all done in jest,
I didn't mean to make you upset.
But I'll give you a go to win back your dough
If you'd just care to make one more bet.

"Now, If you'll go down far to the end of the bar
An' place there a shot glass upright,
I'll make one more bet that you won't regret,
And, most likely, you'll be richer tonight.

"But I'll bet the twenty you had, then ten more I'll add,
I can fill up that shot glass so far
With nothing more than the juice from my lip full of snoose
An' not get one drop on your bar."

Well, the Bartender knew 'twas at least twenty feet
Along that bar made of inlaid hardwood,
And although he'd known men who were good with their aim,
No one was known to be that good.

So he took up the bet and laid down his dough,
The shot glass was placed quick and neat.
Larry stepped up spry, let tobaccer juice fly—
Not a drop came within seven feet.

Larry was beat . . . revenge was sweet,
The 'Keep was laughin', *"I knew it, the target was too far."*
He walked up with a grin, pocketed his win,
Grabbed a rag an' started cleanin' the bar.

"Hey, what's with the grin? You're now into me ten,"
He said, wipin' the bar all the while.
**"Well, I bet my friends where they are, I could spit on your bar,
And you'd wipe it up with a smile."**

When it seems it might be easier not to tell the truth,
Remember—lies, like chickens, usually come back home to roost.

Sentence

NCE upon a time
    in a country very near
Lived a people with a government
    that never had a peer,
For they based their constitution
    on rights of individual man,
Figurin' if there was incentive,
    each would do the best they can;
And in a brief and splendid history,
    they proved that to be true,
And they prospered and they flourished
    and their country grew and grew,
And in their aspirations,
    they sometimes left a rutted track,
And they grieved in anguished sorrow
    when they took time to look back,
For dereliction and destruction
    were left behind them in their wake;
But being smart and good and prudent
    they vowed to do what it would take
To restore, revive, replenish
    all that fell in progress' way,
And they learned repair is costly,
    but someone would have to pay;
So they passed some legislation
    towards the obvious at first,
'Cause the wheel that gets the grease
    is the wheel that squeaks the worst—
But they found that squealin' cylinder
    attached to a great beast
That provided for the masses,
    so their efforts left the East,
And they headed south, but not for long,
    then north to no avail,

For the numbers and the politics
        would prove their efforts fail;
So with sweat and time exhausted,
        they reckoned it'd be best
If they'd throw the blame of all
        on the few who lived out West,
Where miles outnumbered people
        and self-reliance still prevailed,
And the train-of-thought that built the country
        hadn't changed or been derailed,
And they overtook them easily—
        they weren't the type to organize—
But, then, in a few short seasons
        they began to realize
That they hadn't helped the problem;
        fact is, they made it all the worse;
And new sores began to fester,
        infecting everybody's purse—
For they'd lost a needed staple
        and the initial problems took back seat
To the snowballing dilemma
        that would lead to their defeat;
So they tried to turn the clock back,
        but the chain had lost a link,
And it soon became apparent
        that the ship was doomed to sink,
And the country that could've had it all
        would die and fall amiss;
And if there's such thing as a moral,
        I suppose it would be this:
There's some simple truths we can't afford
        to side-step or avoid;
New paint won't save a house
        if the foundation's been destroyed.

Morning Soliloquy

Well, it's time to get up, I reckon.
The new day will soon arrive.
I'll get some coffee in me
An' then maybe I'll revive.

Oh, but it's chilly this mornin'—
Fall always takes its toll—
There's two pot bellies need feedin'—
Mine biscuits, the other one coal.

Prob'ly hafta bust ice to wash up with;
Won't be shavin' whiskers off this ol' chin;
But I'll put some water on the stove
Tonight 'fore I turn in.

I'm out of bacon and sugar—
Been a week since my coffee was sweet.
Thank heaven's I've still got some prunes left;
Without 'em I dare not eat.

My sleep last night was fitful,
What with this tooth an' the knees that pain,
The dreams of the youth I squandered,
An' that pack rat raisin' cain.

Sure don't look forward to saddlin' ol' Brownie;
Cold morns put a hump in his back.
It'll prob'ly take me a while
To get that ol' boy to untrack.

I don't know why I still do it;
Ain't easy on these outfits alone;
But it ain't like I've got many choices—
This lifestyle's all that I've known.

So, I guess I best quit complainin';
It's always paid enough to survive.
An' what the hell, I'll admit it—
It is good just to be alive.

The Gift

I was going through my mom's junk drawer
For somethin' I needed bad
And come across some sure 'nuff treasures—
Things I didn't know she had.

I found a crumpled paper
That made me stop and pause.
'Twas a letter from a six-year-old
To dear old Santa Claus.

It started out plumb reg'lar,
How he'd been good and such,
And the presents he was asking for
Did not amount to much,

'Cuz what he really wanted, you see,
More than a trinket or two,
Was to get ol' Santee to let him be
A real live buckaroo.

He said he didn't know too much
But he was quick to learn,
An' it didn't matter where he'd throw his bed
Or how much dough he'd earn,

Just long as he could ride a horse
And punch cows all his life
And when he grow'd up big like Dad,
He'd want a cowboy wife.

And then it really struck me
When the kid had signed his name
That the author and the reader
Of that letter was the same.

So I sat and wrote a thank you note
To Santa for the gift he'd give
To a child back in '56,
And the life he'd let me live.

Blood, Sweat, and Steers

We were trottin' home for dinner.
Our day, thus far, had been a winner:
We had been turnin' out some pairs on railroad lease.
I's ridin' with ol' Jim,
And if I's asked to describe him
I'd simply say he was a cowboy masterpiece.

We'd stopped to let our horses blow,
When in a canyon down below
We spied a neighbor doin' battle with a steer.
That brute had sulled and brushed-up thick
In some willows near the crick
A full-scale war had been declared and that was clear.

Now I'd had cattle sull on me,
And it was obvious to see
That a reconciliation wouldn't come.
And from experience I knew
If he continued to pursue
That fight, there'd be one of 'em hurt before it's done.

Jim just rolled hisself a smoke
And snickered like it was a joke
While we both sat and watched this feller fight his head.
That cowboy'd cuss an' froth an' yelp,
I asked, "S'pose we should go and help?"
But old Jim then got philosophical and said:

"If he'd just let that brute calm down,
Then bring an old cow back around
That steer would likely follow it to Oregon.
I ain't sayin' it's wrong to fight
If you've got to and your right,
But 'fore you do it's good to know which side yer on.

"Seems, when we were six and nine,
Me and my brother was inclined
To get ourselves in trouble tryin' to be good.
Most times was our fault, sure enough,
But it'd be innocent young kid stuff
That would oftentimes just be misunderstood.

"Like one hot day we'd gone to church
And in a pew we took a perch.
It had been rainin' and the air was thick and wet,
Which made it hard to stay awake;
'Twas about as much as we could take
What with the preachin' and the snorin' and the sweat.

"The gal in front of him and me
Had, well, perspired profusely,
And when she rose, her clothes were clingin', so to speak.
Adding to this situation,
On closer examination,
We saw the dress had lodged itself between her cheeks!

"Sure looked uncomf'terble in there,
We couldn't help ourselves but stare—
An' bein's just waist high, we really saw it good!
Not bein' one to let things be,
My brother pulls that dress out free,
Alleviatin' the whole problem where she stood.

"My brother pulls that dress out free. . . "

"She turns quick an' he just smiled,
Never dreamin' she'd be riled.
But instead of thanks, she hit him with her purse,
Which knocked my brother to the ground;
She glared at me then turned around.
Things were bad, but tryin' to help, I made it worse:

"I know'd somethin' made her mad
To hit my brother like she had,
An' I reckoned it must be the dress, confound it.
So, using sweat marks for a guide
I turns my whole hand on it's side—
And I slips it right back in the way we found it!

"This time 'twas me that felt her wrath
Which knocked my senses off their path,
And I carry purse scars with me to this day.
I guess we got what we were due.
And when we finally came to,
We learned a lesson that I'll share with you today:

" 'Tain't always smart to offer aid
In situations you ain't made.
Experience has taught me not to fight a losing battle.
It's like my daddy always said,
Sometimes best quit while you're ahead,
'Cuz there ain't no reasonin' with wimen or sulled-up cattle!"

Haven't Sold Your Saddle

"Not so terribly well," I said, in answer to his question.
"I'm runnin' fast, but wonder if it's in the wrong direction.
My wife has started gainin' weight and gray shows in her hair;
Her existence seems to be in runnin' kids from here to there.

"My job has lost its challenge; it seems like it never changes.
Sometimes I'd like to chuck it all and leave to ride new ranges."
I thought my friend would understand; he'd walked this same ol' road
And had made decisions in his life to drop his heavy load.

So, I laid my troubles on him and I told him how I felt.
He just stares at me, all hollow, like he's hit below the belt.
He sits down close, all weak-like, and he looks me in the eye.
His hands, they started tremblin', I believes he's gonna cry.

He swallows hard an' tells me, "I know what you're up against;
It happens at this time of life. You feel like you've been fenced.
Seems like life becomes routine . . . it all just feels the same,
So, you go to huntin' witches, lookin' for someone to blame.

"Our work and wife scapegoat real well when we are of that mind,
And little faults become big, 'cuz, that is what we want to find.
Please don't make my same mistakes and let a notion be your guide.
The grass ain't greener, I see that—now I'm on the other side.

"I upturned several lives with my leaving, plus my own,
An' lost my common little family and my routine little home.
I'd have never left if I had taken time to figure out
That what I wanted out of, is what life is all about.

"We're seldom taught that, though; seems it's almost out of style.
If I could just have one more chance, I'd walk that extra mile.
But that can't be, now I must lie upon the bed I've made
While my will to carry on, like bad memories, starts to fade.

"And if you never take advice again, please heed these words, my friend:
The purpose of life's race is in the running to the end.
There will be times it seems so far we fear we'll never make it;
We tire and lose sight of dreams and want to just forsake it.

"It's still all in your mind right now, but thought precedes the act.
And it isn't yet too late, my friend—I know that for a fact.
You've started your race gamely. You've just been bumped against the rail.
I'm not sayin' you sold your saddle, but you've put it up for sale."

I surely don't know all the answers—
And I have no problem with that.
If I did, I'd quit this cowboy life
And become a bureaucrat!

Pick-up-acality

Most folks have the luxury of choosing what they drive,
Be it basic transportation or a motor car they prize;
They can own a van or wagon or a sporty little coupe.
They've a vast array of choices in the way that they commute.

But when it comes to vehicles, a cowboy's sort of stuck.
He can choose who's going to make it, but it's got to be a truck.
It's the way he lives that dictates what he needs to get him by,
And I think that you will notice that most of them comply.

He needs a truck to haul the hay to feed his ol' cayuse,
And he lives on roads where seedans cannot take that much abuse.
Then in spring and fall, when it comes time to buckaroo,
He will need to load his tack and camp to meet the round-up crew.

He needs a truck for fencin', to haul the wire and the posts.
But none of that's the reason that he needs a truck the most.
And what I'm going to tell you now is really where it's at:
He needs to drive a pickup 'cuz there's room to wear his hat!

When they brag on themselves, but of others
They've never a kind word to say,
I always chalk it up to the fact that
An ass loves to hear himself bray!

What Will I Tell Him?

What will I tell him, you ask me,
When my son's trying to make up his mind?
To ride for a living like I have,
Or explore what the world has to find?
Could I tell him it's sure worth the doing?
Could I tell him I spent well my time?
I'll just say from the start,
Son, it's gotta come from the heart;
It ain't something that comes from the mind.

I'll tell him the truth as I know it—
Of good years, hard winters and drought.
The ecstasy of winning a round now and then,
Givin' courage to stay in the bout.
That adrenaline rush when you're bustin' up brush
On a cowpony, agile and stout,
Of havin' the rug jerked from under your feet
When you hear that the outfit's sold out.

I'll tell him that cowboy's a verb, not a noun:
It's what you do more than a name.
And he'd be foolin' himself if he's figurin' on
Any sort of material gain.
I'll remind him of spring calves a-buckin',
Of the joy and the pride and the pain
Of livin' a life that is easy or hard
At the discretion at nature's refrain.

What will I tell him, you ask me,
When he's there and tryin' to make up his mind?
I'll just say from the start,
Son, it's gotta come from the heart;
It ain't something that comes from the mind.

Moments of Rapture

Would you mind sittin' down?
I've got thoughts runnin' 'round
In my head that I'd like to get out.
If you'll listen to me
As I set some thoughts free,
You'll soon know what this is about.
Now, I've been through a bunch
And I've got a good hunch
That I ain't seen the last of hard times,
'Cuz there's bound to be more
'Fore they tally the score
And I'm laid in a box made of pine.

The prices I've paid
For mistakes that I've made
Have rendered me wary but wise,
And I've endured pain
That near drove me insane—
You've said that it shows in my eyes.
With a heavy remorse,
I've seen death and divorce
And goals scattered like chaff in the gale.
So I put up my guard,
Turned inward and hard
And quit tryin' so I wouldn't fail.

But then I met you and believe it is true
That fate had a role in this hand,
And emotions I'd taken for dead reawakened
And blossomed within me again.

And my mind flashes moments of rapture.
I believe my heart's pleading for me
To unlock the gate before it's too late
To set pain and bitterness free.

And my mind flashes moments of rapture.
Your hug or your kiss or your touch,
An innocent glance or a brushing by chance—
And the past doesn't matter so much.

There are those who will just refuse
To play the hand they're dealt.
But a cheater's like a dead cat—
He ain't worth his own stretched pelt.

Which Side?

The argument we'll now address
Has been going on for years,
With debates among great scholars
And harsh words between my peers—

A philosophical question,
Contemplating right from wrong,
Dealing with the proper side to
Have your spur strap buckle on.

There are those who claim "tradition,"
For others it's "common sense,"
Some cite "practicality"—
Almost no one rides the fence.

But the truth—though I am sure there's
Those among you who will scoff—
Is that a spur strap's merely there
To keep your spurs from falling off!

"There are those who claim 'tradition' . . ."

The Book

Not so awful long ago,
Before I married Toot
An' settled down an' had some kids,
I wore a fancy boot
An' rode with the big outfits
Thet pulled the wagon out.
An' ropin' cows an' ridin' broncs
Was all I cared about.

But even then the winters came,
An' then a buckaroo
Would have to hunt him up a job
To spend the winter through.
An' so I took a line camp,
'Twas better then feedin' hay,
An' that's kinda where my story starts,
On a cold December day.

We're camped there over two months now,
With nary time to play,
A-ridin' fence an' spreadin' salt
An' watchin' cows don't stray.
An' I'm feelin' purty sorry
For this feller known as me,
'Cuz I'm out here an' town's in there—
An' that's abotherin' me.

Stub gets up an' starts a fire,
Rubs his frost-bit toes.
"The only place we'll sweat today
Is underneath the nose."
It's the twenty-fifth day of December,
The thermometer shows ten below.
The wind is blow'n from the north,
The clouds are threatenin' snow.

I pulls out of my bedroll
An' dresses to fight the cold.
Stub steps out to use the outhouse
An' I thinks to m'self, "How bold."
I goes down an' grains the horses,
Chops the ice an' then some wood;
And when I gets back to the cabin,
Stub's got breakfast smellin' good.

We sit down to biscuits an' gravy,
Venison steaks an' black, hot brew.
Not too much conversation
Could be heard between us two:
I had reached the age of twenty-one
An' was a wild buckaroo;
Stub couldn't have realized how I felt—
He was an old man, he's forty-two.

"It just ain't fair I'm stuck out here,"
I finally up and say.
"I should be in ol' Elko town
Learnin' girlies how to play.
Celebratin' Christmas proper.
Like them city people do,
Instead of bein' stuck out here
With no one else but you."

A grin come over his snow-burnt face
As he takes a sip of brew, and says,
"If you'll let me, Old Grandpa here
Might say a word or two.
Now, I know this here is Christmas,
An' you feel you have no chance
To celebrate it proper
Or attend the Christmas dance.

"This ain't my first line-camp job,
But I remember how it felt
The first time thet I just had beans
'Stead 'a turkey 'neath my belt.
An' how no family nor friends were there
To help celebrate the day,
To drink the whiskey, exchange some gifts,
An' while the hours away.

"But then I got to thinkin'
An' I asked myself right out,
'Is this the way we celebrate the day
What Christmas is all about?'
An' I concluded that although it's merry
To laugh, exchange gifts an' such,
If we don't give as much time to the Savior,
The day hasn't gained us too much."

Now I didn't think Stub was no heathen,
But I'd never heard him talk like that,
As if he was religious
Or believed in stuff like that.
I probably looked kind'er silly,
'Cuz it took me by surprise,
A him a talkin' out like that.
An' he could see it in my eyes.

He said, "What's the matter, boy?
Don't you believe the Good Book's true?"
I said "I never give it much thought . . .
Why? . . . Do you?"
"Well, I have some trouble read'n it—
The way them fellers write;
But it makes me feel real good inside,
Like I'm doin' somethin' right.

"An' anyone in our occupation,
See'n the things that cowboys see,
Must know there's a whole lot more out there—
Somethin' much bigger than he—
Providin' water an' grasses,
Mountains an' trees an' air,
A place for a calf to grow big an' fat
An' a reason for man to be there.

"And the way I got it figured,
Celebratin' Christmas should be two-fold:
Part for family, gifts an' friends,
An' part for the Book of Old.
"An' seein' as how it's just you an' me
An' the beans an' the coffee stout,
Well, the family an' friends,
An' the turkey an' trims, we'll have to do without.

But as far as celebratin' the day of the birth
Of the Atonin' One,
I think it proper thet you an' me
Set an' read on the Bible some."
So after the daily duties was done
An' the beans was in the pot,
We sat an' read us some of that book—
I don't remember jist what—

But it had to do with the birth of the Lord,
Some wise men an' shepherds an' such,
An' I've heard the story a number of times since
But I never enjoyed it so much.
But that day, as now an' always,
Not just to be the man's dub,
It made me feel real good inside—
An' I'll always thank you for that, Stub.

Pun-ishment

Some cowboys hired out one time.
What they learned ain't found on page:
They'd gone to work for old Jake Grime,
But never drew their summer wage.

Jake's range was what you'd call immense;
It covered many desolate miles,
With no corral or trap or fence.
They rode until they all got piles.

Grime's cattle were all fast and big,
Which made the gather wild and hard.
An' all they et was boil'd pig
Until the whole crew sweat pure lard.

But after three months to the day,
They finally got the work all done
And turned to Jake to draw their pay
To go to town for rest and fun.

Grimes looked plumb sad, says "Shucks and joys,"
As if they'd hurt him deep inside,
"There's folks back East pays big bucks, boys,
To go on western horseback rides."

" 'Twas me thet furnished horse an' cow,
And let you ride o'er God's creation;
And most folks would allow as how
You just spent three months' free vacation.

"Just look down at them legs you got
And see how they're so nicely bowed
That there is somethin' cain't be bought!
I reckon how it's me that's owed!"

With pistol lead they drilled him through;
Weren't no hesitance or pauses,
An' natcherly that kilt him too,
So death was listed "natural causes."

They dug his grave down fifty feet,
And if you'd ask them cowboys "why,"
It's 'cuz they figured, way down deep,
He might just be a real fine guy.

They're satisfied how things turned out
And what they learned that fateful day,
'Cuz now they know without a doubt
That it is true, folks, Grime don't pay!

The Experience of Life

Oh, it's the differences we face
    That keep us driven.
And as for troubles 'long the way,
    Well, they're a given.
But it's those opposites in life—
Both the pleasures and the strife—
That can make this ol' life
    Worth the livin'.

I've often wondered why it takes
All these scars for us to learn.
It seems we can't relate to hot
Until our fingers have been burned.
Like cream destined to be butter,
First we've got to take our turn
Through the churn of the experience of life.

We can't judge the weight of burden
'Til we've packed a heavy load,
Haven't tasted apple pie
Until we've tried it à la mode,
And won't appreciate the ride
'Til we've been bucked off on the road
And broke the code to the experience of life.

And it's those differences we face
    That keep us driven.
And as for the troubles 'long the way,
    Well, they're a given.
But in those opposites of life,
    Between the pleasures and the strife,
We can make this ol' life worth the livin'.

We can't tell the worth of pleasure
Without knowing first of pain.
And if we're truly to forgive,
Sometime we've had to bear the blame.
If we don't know firsthand of loss,
How are we going to measure gain
To win the game of the experience of life?

To understand the concept *salty*
We must first have tasted salt.
We won't comprehend perfection
'Til we recognize there's fault.
If we're not willing to roll with it
And we bring it to a halt
We'll lock the vault on the experience of life.

'Cause it's those diff'rences we face
        That keep us driven.
And we know troubles 'long the way
        Will be a given.
But it's those opposites in life—
        Both the pleasures and the strife—
That make this ol' life worth the livin'.

My friend showed up at a rodeo
In a silk shirt, bright colored and frilly.
I said, "Why don't you just wear some sequins?"
He said, "Heck no, that would look silly!"

The Throw-Back

'Twas the end of the nineteenth century
When the cowboy era peaked,
An' a motley clan of horseback men
Perfected a technique
Of handlin' an movin' cattle,
A type raised primarily for meat,
Thus insurin' a hungry young nation
There would always be plenty to eat.

But this entailed a great deal more
Than most people are led to believe,
For in that time an' circumstance,
Nine hundred miles was hard to conceive.

But that's what they were up against
With this long-horned bovine beast,
For the product was in the expanse of the West
And the market was in the East.

Now the problem was gettin' the product to market
At a price all parties could pay,
So, unlike Europe, where only royalty ate meat,
The common man could have beef every day.

But the obstacles seemed near insurmountable,
For the miles between were not kind.
There were rivers to swim an' deserts to cross,
An' water and forage to find
To keep the animals strong and healthy
So they could walk twenty miles a day
An' get to the railway before the snow flew,
To be loaded and shipped on their way.

"He'd have to savvy the ropes . . ."

Now to do this they'd have to be able
To hire a man who would sleep on the ground
For seven long months out of one given year
For forty a month and found.

He'd have to own a few necessities,
Like a saddle that cost at least two months' pay,
A bridle, a bedroll, a slicker, some chaps,
Some spurs an' a mouth harp to play.

He'd have to accept varied menus,
Like biscuits an' beans an' meat,
Or meat an' beans an' biscuits
With coffee throw'd in for a treat.

He'd have to enjoy the great outdoors,
'Cause that's where he'd be night an' day,
Except for the time he'd be behind bars
In some little town 'long the way.

He'd have to be a high-skilled technician,
Fulfill his job atop a low-bred feen,
Leave camp in the morn, make it back in at night,
An' get somethin' done in between.

He would have to savvy the rope,
Be proficient with his lariat skill,
For the man who can't handle this basic job,
His worth to the outfit is nil.

Now you'd think with this list of requirements
That the job would've been hard to fill,
But the human race breeds a throw-back,
And for some reason these men fit the bill.

So through the years cowboys managed
To keep beef in the stores to be bought,
An' the job requirements have changed some
'Cause our country has grown up a lot.

Oh, we still have some of their problems;
Mother Nature still kicks at our rumps.
The job will never be conducive to comfort,
But you learn not to notice the bumps.

But nowadays they've throw'd us some ringers,
New problems that's kicked in our slats,
Like computers, the futures and unions,
And worst of all—bureaucrats.

And the human race still breeds a throw-back,
From their predecessor's mold they are poured,
And they're still puttin' beef in the market
That the common man can afford.

But I can't see that lastin' forever,
For we keep gettin' kicked in the teeth,
An' if you don't think you're gettin' a bargain, Pard,
Just go abroad an' order some beef.

Saddle Tramp Philosopher

We were brandin' Zaga's cattle
At Frost Canyon in the spring,
When neighboring with each other
Was still such a normal thing
That a fella never realized that
The use of this practical tool
In twenty years would be an exception
And not the common rule.

The wives were all at the cabin
Visitin' and cookin' a feast
That'd be served up on long tables with benches
When the sun had moved from the east.
Everyone else was down at the trap
In the dust, and the wind, and the sun,
In unwashed Levi's and sweat-stained hats,
Teachin' me that work can be fun.

From the west a rider came,
Leadin' a packhorse towards camp.
Dad put his hand on my shoulder
And said, "Son, there's the last saddle tramp."
To the mind of this thirteen-year-old,
That was romantic as hell.
He rode up to the herd to visit with Fred,
And I learned his name was Thomas O'Dell.

He asked Fred permission to camp a few days,
Rest his horses, mend a sawbuck.
He was told he was welcome; there was grain in the barn,
And we'd soon all be sittin' to chuck.
Well, we'd finished the brandin', washed at the crick,
And was huntin' some shade and a drink,
When Tom yelled out loud,
"Fred, your outhouse is locked!"
Then just stood there and squinted and blinked.

Fred pulled out a key, threw it to Tom,
Said, "You know, vandals, insurance and such,
They've broke all the dishes, and shot out the phone.
We just can't be here that much."
But Tom wasn't about to let this thing drop.
He kept standin' there blinkin' his eyes.
I recognize now that's the cue that he'd give
Just before he philosophized.

He said, "Fred, my granddaddy, Lord rest his soul,
Took a homestead in what's now Arkansas.
And the first thing he done was to dig a deep hole
And take lumber he'd cut from the raw,
And built him a three-holer privy,
One that'd stand through the good times and bad.
And for thirty years, Fred, he never locked the door once,
Then he turned the place over to Dad.

Then through the depression Dad raised us kids.
There were times we didn't have a dime.
But unlocked, it stood there through famine and flood,
Even through green-apple time.
Now my brother runs that outfit, and has for thirty-odd years,
And that outhouse is still used regular—
Unlocked, I have little fear."

About now Fred says, "Tom, don't you see?
It's really not that big a deal.
It's just that these vandals from town will tear up
Anything that ain't handy to steal."
But Tom just kept squintin' and blinkin',
And scratchin' his head 'neath his hat.
We were all on our toes to hear what he'd say next,
And he was relishing that.

Then he looked at that ground he'd been toein',
Said, "Fred, I'd bet my good horseshoein' anvil
That in the seventy-five years that outhouse stood there—
No one ever stole as much as one handful!"

Little Bull

My story is of three bulls,
All of a bovine breed,
Who were travelin' the desert together
In search of a little feed,

When on a knoll they came upon
A meadow a spring had made,
With bright, green grass and trees about
That allowed for a little shade.

Now, the largest of the three bulls
Bowed his neck, and snot was blown,
Which was warnin' enough for the smaller two
That he wanted this place for his own.

So now there are two bulls travelin'
In search of a place to stop
To fill up on green grass and water—
Which they found on a mountain top.

This place suited both bulls to a tee,
But as oft happens, as history will show,
The larger bull thumped the smaller one good,
So back on the trail he would go.

Now, my story has a moral—
One I hope you'll learn today—
And it's that sometimes . . . a little bull
Will go a long . . . long way.

Evening Chat

Here you go, young feller.
Let me take this saddle off your back.
I'll get a scoop of rolled oats
And we'll have us an evening chat.

Now let me curry this sweat off,
I suppose it's the least I can do.
Settle down now, enjoy your grain;
I'll turn you out when you're through.

Well, we finished us up another day.
That ol' sun is going down.
Hmmmph, I wonder why we say that,
When it's the earth that's spun around.

'Cause the sun is stationary, you see, it's the earth . . .
. . . What's that, boredom in your eyes?
I guess it don't make no difference to you
If we call it "sundown" or "earthrise."

But regardless, we had us a good day,
And got what I wanted to done;
Neither one of us got hurt,
And we managed to have us some fun.

Got me high hopes for you, Brownie.
I believe we'll make a good team.
You've just gotta slow down a little;
In time you'll know what I mean.

When I was young I was like you,
But when working cows, you'll find
That enthusiasm's dandy,
But experience is kind.

"Settle down now, enjoy your grain."

It sorta lets an older feller
Work at a slower pace
And still get as much accomplished—
On account of fewer mistakes.

Here, let me have your foot up;
I'll check on that ol' hoof crack.
Hold yourself up, darn it,
No need to be hard on my back.

Yep, them clips I drew have done it.
Looks like it's growing out fine.
Won't hardly know you had one
When I shoe you up next time.

Say, but you caught that yearling slick.
Do you like ropin' as much as you claim to?
Maybe we should enter us a jackpot—
Now there'd be something to aim to.

But I don't see the boss allowin'
Me to take you past them hills.
'Sides, you know nothing of trailerin'
And I don't reckon you ever will.

See, you and I are a dying breed.
Ain't many left like us these days.
Well, I see you've et up the last of your grain,
Come on, pard, you go out and graze.

Thanks for the chat, I've enjoyed it.
S'pose I'd best head on inside
And git me some supper started.
Catch ya later, pard. . . . Thanks for the ride.

A cowboy poem's a photo
Of a life spent on the range,
With a philosophy on livin',
Citin' ethics, work and change—
Vignettes of life uncompromised
By power, fad, or greed,
Written by a horseback author
Livin' by the West's own creed.